Thank you for your support of **"Recipe Blank Book"** throughout the years. We are proud of your enthusiasm to make great things in the kitchen.

RECIPE

DATE : _____

TITLE : _____

PREP TIME : _____

COOK TIME : _____

INGREDIENTS :

_____

_____

_____

_____

_____

_____

_____

_____

_____

_____

_____

_____

_____

_____

DIRECTIONS :

_____

_____

_____

_____

_____

_____

_____

_____

_____

_____

NOTES

_____

_____

_____

_____

RECIPE

DATE : _____

TITLE : _____

PREP TIME : _____

COOK TIME : _____

INGREDIENTS :

_____

_____

_____

_____

_____

_____

_____

_____

_____

_____

_____

_____

_____

_____

DIRECTIONS :

_____

_____

_____

_____

_____

_____

_____

_____

_____

_____

NOTES

_____

_____

_____

_____

RECIPE

DATE : _____

TITLE : _____

PREP TIME : _____

COOK TIME : _____

INGREDIENTS :

_____

_____

_____

_____

_____

_____

_____

_____

_____

_____

_____

_____

_____

_____

_____

_____

DIRECTIONS :

_____

_____

_____

_____

_____

_____

_____

_____

_____

_____

_____

_____

NOTES

_____

_____

_____

_____

RECIPE

DATE : _____

TITLE : _____

PREP TIME : _____

COOK TIME : _____

INGREDIENTS :

_____

_____

_____

_____

_____

_____

_____

_____

_____

_____

_____

_____

_____

_____

_____

_____

DIRECTIONS :

_____

_____

_____

_____

_____

_____

_____

_____

_____

_____

_____

NOTES

_____

_____

_____

RECIPE

DATE : _____

TITLE : _____

PREP TIME : _____

COOK TIME : _____

INGREDIENTS :

_____

_____

_____

_____

_____

_____

_____

_____

_____

_____

_____

_____

_____

_____

_____

_____

DIRECTIONS :

_____

_____

_____

_____

_____

_____

_____

_____

_____

_____

_____

NOTES

_____

_____

_____

_____

RECIPE

DATE : _____

TITLE : _____

PREP TIME : _____

COOK TIME : _____

INGREDIENTS :

_____
_____
_____
_____
_____
_____
_____
_____
_____
_____
_____
_____
_____
_____
_____

DIRECTIONS :

_____
_____
_____
_____
_____
_____
_____
_____
_____
_____

NOTES

_____
_____
_____
_____

RECIPE

DATE : _____

TITLE : _____

PREP TIME : _____

COOK TIME : _____

INGREDIENTS :

_____

_____

_____

_____

_____

_____

_____

_____

_____

_____

_____

_____

_____

DIRECTIONS :

_____

_____

_____

_____

_____

_____

_____

_____

_____

_____

NOTES

_____

_____

_____

_____

RECIPE

DATE : _____

TITLE : _____

PREP TIME : _____

COOK TIME : _____

INGREDIENTS :

_____

_____

_____

_____

_____

_____

_____

_____

_____

_____

_____

_____

_____

_____

_____

_____

DIRECTIONS :

_____

_____

_____

_____

_____

_____

_____

_____

_____

NOTES

_____

_____

_____

_____

RECIPE

DATE : _____

TITLE : _____

PREP TIME : _____

COOK TIME : _____

INGREDIENTS :

_____

_____

_____

_____

_____

_____

_____

_____

_____

_____

_____

_____

_____

DIRECTIONS :

_____

_____

_____

_____

_____

_____

_____

_____

_____

_____

NOTES

_____

_____

_____

_____

RECIPE

DATE : _____

TITLE : _____

PREP TIME : _____

COOK TIME : _____

INGREDIENTS :

_____

_____

_____

_____

_____

_____

_____

_____

_____

_____

_____

_____

_____

_____

DIRECTIONS :

_____

_____

_____

_____

_____

_____

_____

_____

_____

_____

_____

NOTES

_____

_____

_____

_____

RECIPE

DATE : _____

TITLE : _____

PREP TIME : _____

COOK TIME : _____

INGREDIENTS :

_____

_____

_____

_____

_____

_____

_____

_____

_____

_____

_____

_____

_____

_____

DIRECTIONS :

_____

_____

_____

_____

_____

_____

_____

_____

_____

_____

_____

NOTES

_____

_____

_____

_____

RECIPE

DATE : _____

TITLE : _____

PREP TIME : _____

COOK TIME : _____

INGREDIENTS :

_____

_____

_____

_____

_____

_____

_____

_____

_____

_____

_____

_____

_____

_____

_____

_____

DIRECTIONS :

_____

_____

_____

_____

_____

_____

_____

_____

_____

_____

NOTES

_____

_____

_____

_____

RECIPE

DATE : _____

TITLE : _____

PREP TIME : _____

COOK TIME : _____

INGREDIENTS :

_____
_____
_____
_____
_____
_____
_____
_____
_____
_____
_____
_____
_____
_____

DIRECTIONS :

_____
_____
_____
_____
_____
_____
_____
_____
_____
_____

NOTES

_____
_____
_____
_____

RECIPE

DATE : _____

TITLE : _____

PREP TIME : _____

COOK TIME : _____

INGREDIENTS :

_____

_____

_____

_____

_____

_____

_____

_____

_____

_____

_____

_____

_____

_____

_____

_____

_____

DIRECTIONS :

_____

_____

_____

_____

_____

_____

_____

_____

_____

_____

_____

_____

NOTES

_____

_____

_____

_____

RECIPE

DATE : _____

TITLE : _____

PREP TIME : _____

COOK TIME : _____

INGREDIENTS :

_____

_____

_____

_____

_____

_____

_____

_____

_____

_____

_____

_____

_____

_____

_____

. _____

DIRECTIONS :

_____

_____

_____

_____

_____

_____

_____

_____

_____

_____

_____

NOTES

_____

_____

_____

_____

RECIPE

DATE : _____

TITLE : _____

PREP TIME : _____

COOK TIME : _____

INGREDIENTS :

_____

_____

_____

_____

_____

_____

_____

_____

_____

_____

_____

_____

_____

_____

_____

_____

DIRECTIONS :

_____

_____

_____

_____

_____

_____

_____

_____

_____

_____

NOTES

_____

_____

_____

RECIPE

DATE : _____

TITLE : _____

PREP TIME : _____

COOK TIME : _____

INGREDIENTS :

_____

_____

_____

_____

_____

_____

_____

_____

_____

_____

_____

_____

_____

_____

_____

DIRECTIONS :

_____

_____

_____

_____

_____

_____

_____

_____

_____

_____

_____

_____

NOTES

_____

_____

_____

_____

RECIPE

DATE : _____

TITLE : _____

PREP TIME : _____

COOK TIME : _____

INGREDIENTS :

_____

_____

_____

_____

_____

_____

_____

_____

_____

_____

_____

_____

_____

_____

_____

_____

_____

DIRECTIONS :

_____

_____

_____

_____

_____

_____

_____

_____

_____

_____

_____

_____

NOTES

_____

_____

_____

_____

RECIPE

DATE : _____

TITLE : _____

PREP TIME : _____

COOK TIME : _____

INGREDIENTS :

_____

_____

_____

_____

_____

_____

_____

_____

_____

_____

_____

_____

_____

_____

_____

_____

_____

DIRECTIONS :

_____

_____

_____

_____

_____

_____

_____

_____

_____

_____

_____

_____

NOTES

_____

_____

_____

_____

RECIPE

DATE : _____

TITLE : _____

PREP TIME : _____

COOK TIME : _____

INGREDIENTS :

_____
_____
_____
_____
_____
_____
_____
_____
_____
_____
_____
_____
_____
_____
_____
_____
_____

DIRECTIONS :

_____
_____
_____
_____
_____
_____
_____
_____
_____
_____
_____
_____

NOTES

_____
_____
_____
_____

RECIPE

DATE : _____

TITLE : _____

PREP TIME : _____

COOK TIME : _____

INGREDIENTS :

_____

_____

_____

_____

_____

_____

_____

_____

_____

_____

_____

_____

_____

_____

_____

DIRECTIONS :

_____

_____

_____

_____

_____

_____

_____

_____

_____

_____

_____

NOTES

_____

_____

_____

_____

RECIPE

DATE : _____

TITLE : _____

PREP TIME : _____

COOK TIME : _____

INGREDIENTS :

_____

_____

_____

_____

_____

_____

_____

_____

_____

_____

_____

_____

_____

_____

_____

_____

DIRECTIONS :

_____

_____

_____

_____

_____

_____

_____

_____

_____

_____

_____

NOTES

_____

_____

_____

_____

RECIPE

DATE : _____

TITLE : _____

PREP TIME : _____

COOK TIME : _____

INGREDIENTS :

_____

_____

_____

_____

_____

_____

_____

_____

_____

_____

_____

_____

_____

_____

_____

_____

_____

DIRECTIONS :

_____

_____

_____

_____

_____

_____

_____

_____

_____

_____

_____

_____

NOTES

_____

_____

_____

_____

RECIPE

DATE : _____

TITLE : _____

PREP TIME : _____

COOK TIME : _____

INGREDIENTS :

_____

_____

_____

_____

_____

_____

_____

_____

_____

_____

_____

_____

_____

_____

_____

DIRECTIONS :

_____

_____

_____

_____

_____

_____

_____

_____

_____

_____

_____

NOTES

_____

_____

_____

_____

RECIPE

DATE : _____

TITLE : _____

PREP TIME : _____

COOK TIME : _____

INGREDIENTS :

_____

_____

_____

_____

_____

_____

_____

_____

_____

_____

_____

_____

_____

_____

DIRECTIONS :

_____

_____

_____

_____

_____

_____

_____

_____

_____

_____

_____

NOTES

_____

_____

_____

_____

RECIPE

DATE : _____

TITLE : _____

PREP TIME : _____

COOK TIME : _____

INGREDIENTS :

_____

_____

_____

_____

_____

_____

_____

_____

_____

_____

_____

_____

_____

_____

_____

_____

DIRECTIONS :

_____

_____

_____

_____

_____

_____

_____

_____

_____

_____

_____

_____

NOTES

_____

_____

_____

_____

RECIPE

DATE : _____

TITLE : _____

PREP TIME : _____

COOK TIME : _____

INGREDIENTS :

_____

_____

_____

_____

_____

_____

_____

_____

_____

_____

_____

_____

_____

_____

_____

_____

DIRECTIONS :

_____

_____

_____

_____

_____

_____

_____

_____

_____

_____

_____

_____

NOTES

_____

_____

_____

_____

RECIPE

DATE : _____

TITLE : _____

PREP TIME : _____

COOK TIME : _____

INGREDIENTS :

_____

_____

_____

_____

_____

_____

_____

_____

_____

_____

_____

_____

_____

_____

DIRECTIONS :

_____

_____

_____

_____

_____

_____

_____

_____

_____

_____

NOTES

_____

_____

_____

_____

RECIPE

DATE : _____

TITLE : _____

PREP TIME : _____

COOK TIME : _____

INGREDIENTS :

_____

_____

_____

_____

_____

_____

_____

_____

_____

_____

_____

_____

_____

_____

DIRECTIONS :

_____

_____

_____

_____

_____

_____

_____

_____

_____

_____

_____

NOTES

_____

_____

_____

RECIPE

DATE : _____

TITLE : _____

PREP TIME : _____

COOK TIME : _____

INGREDIENTS :

_____

_____

_____

_____

_____

_____

_____

_____

_____

_____

_____

_____

_____

_____

_____

_____

DIRECTIONS :

_____

_____

_____

_____

_____

_____

_____

_____

_____

_____

_____

_____

NOTES

_____

_____

_____

_____

RECIPE

DATE : _____

TITLE : _____

PREP TIME : _____

COOK TIME : _____

INGREDIENTS :

_____

_____

_____

_____

_____

_____

_____

_____

_____

_____

_____

_____

_____

_____

_____

DIRECTIONS :

_____

_____

_____

_____

_____

_____

_____

_____

_____

_____

_____

_____

NOTES

_____

_____

_____

_____

RECIPE

DATE : _____

TITLE : _____

PREP TIME : _____

COOK TIME : _____

INGREDIENTS :

_____

_____

_____

_____

_____

_____

_____

_____

_____

_____

_____

_____

_____

_____

_____

_____

DIRECTIONS :

_____

_____

_____

_____

_____

_____

_____

_____

_____

_____

_____

NOTES

_____

_____

_____

_____

RECIPE

DATE : _____

TITLE : _____

PREP TIME : _____

COOK TIME : _____

INGREDIENTS :

_____

_____

_____

_____

_____

_____

_____

_____

_____

_____

_____

_____

_____

_____

_____

_____

DIRECTIONS :

_____

_____

_____

_____

_____

_____

_____

_____

_____

_____

NOTES

_____

_____

_____

_____

RECIPE

DATE : _____

TITLE : _____

PREP TIME : _____

COOK TIME : _____

INGREDIENTS :

_____

_____

_____

_____

_____

_____

_____

_____

_____

_____

_____

_____

_____

_____

_____

_____

_____

DIRECTIONS :

_____

_____

_____

_____

_____

_____

_____

_____

_____

_____

_____

NOTES

_____

_____

_____

_____

RECIPE

DATE : _____

TITLE : _____

PREP TIME : _____

COOK TIME : _____

INGREDIENTS :

_____

_____

_____

_____

_____

_____

_____

_____

_____

_____

_____

_____

_____

_____

_____

_____

DIRECTIONS :

_____

_____

_____

_____

_____

_____

_____

_____

_____

_____

_____

NOTES

_____

_____

_____

_____

RECIPE

DATE : _____

TITLE : _____

PREP TIME : _____

COOK TIME : _____

INGREDIENTS :

_____

_____

_____

_____

_____

_____

_____

_____

_____

_____

_____

_____

_____

_____

_____

DIRECTIONS :

_____

_____

_____

_____

_____

_____

_____

_____

_____

_____

_____

NOTES

_____

_____

_____

_____

RECIPE

DATE : _____

TITLE : _____

PREP TIME : _____

COOK TIME : _____

INGREDIENTS :

_____

_____

_____

_____

_____

_____

_____

_____

_____

_____

_____

_____

_____

_____

DIRECTIONS :

_____

_____

_____

_____

_____

_____

_____

_____

_____

_____

_____

NOTES

_____

_____

_____

_____

RECIPE

DATE : _____

TITLE : _____

PREP TIME : _____

COOK TIME : _____

INGREDIENTS :

_____
_____
_____
_____
_____
_____
_____
_____
_____
_____
_____
_____
_____
_____
_____
_____

DIRECTIONS :

_____
_____
_____
_____
_____
_____
_____
_____
_____
_____
_____
_____

NOTES

_____
_____
_____
_____

RECIPE

DATE : _____

TITLE : _____

PREP TIME : _____

COOK TIME : _____

INGREDIENTS :

_____

_____

_____

_____

_____

_____

_____

_____

_____

_____

_____

_____

_____

_____

_____

_____

DIRECTIONS :

_____

_____

_____

_____

_____

_____

_____

_____

_____

_____

_____

NOTES

_____

_____

_____

_____

RECITE

DATE : _____

TITLE : _____

PREP TIME : _____

COOK TIME : _____

INGREDIENTS :

_____
_____
_____
_____
_____
_____
_____
_____
_____
_____
_____
_____
_____
_____
_____

DIRECTIONS :

_____
_____
_____
_____
_____
_____
_____
_____
_____
_____
_____

NOTES

_____
_____
_____
_____

RECIPE

DATE : _____

TITLE : _____

PREP TIME : _____

COOK TIME : _____

INGREDIENTS :

_____

_____

_____

_____

_____

_____

_____

_____

_____

_____

_____

_____

_____

_____

_____

DIRECTIONS :

_____

_____

_____

_____

_____

_____

_____

_____

_____

_____

_____

NOTES

_____

_____

_____

_____

RECIPE

DATE : _____

TITLE : _____

PREP TIME : _____

COOK TIME : _____

INGREDIENTS :

_____

_____

_____

_____

_____

_____

_____

_____

_____

_____

_____

_____

_____

_____

_____

_____

DIRECTIONS :

_____

_____

_____

_____

_____

_____

_____

_____

_____

_____

NOTES

_____

_____

_____

RECIPE

DATE : _____

TITLE : _____

PREP TIME : _____

COOK TIME : _____

INGREDIENTS :

_____

_____

_____

_____

_____

_____

_____

_____

_____

_____

_____

_____

_____

_____

_____

_____

DIRECTIONS :

_____

_____

_____

_____

_____

_____

_____

_____

_____

_____

_____

NOTES

_____

_____

_____

_____

RECIPE

DATE : _____

TITLE : _____

PREP TIME : _____

COOK TIME : _____

INGREDIENTS :

_____

_____

_____

_____

_____

_____

_____

_____

_____

_____

_____

_____

_____

_____

_____

DIRECTIONS :

_____

_____

_____

_____

_____

_____

_____

_____

_____

_____

NOTES

_____

_____

_____

_____

RECIPE

DATE : _____

TITLE : _____

PREP TIME : _____

COOK TIME : _____

INGREDIENTS :

_____

_____

_____

_____

_____

_____

_____

_____

_____

_____

_____

_____

_____

_____

_____

DIRECTIONS :

_____

_____

_____

_____

_____

_____

_____

_____

_____

_____

_____

NOTES

_____

_____

_____

_____

RECIPE

DATE : _____

TITLE : _____

PREP TIME : _____

COOK TIME : _____

INGREDIENTS :

_____

_____

_____

_____

_____

_____

_____

_____

_____

_____

_____

_____

_____

_____

_____

_____

DIRECTIONS :

_____

_____

_____

_____

_____

_____

_____

_____

_____

_____

_____

NOTES

_____

_____

_____

_____

RECIPE

DATE : _____

TITLE : _____

PREP TIME : _____

COOK TIME : _____

INGREDIENTS :

_____

_____

_____

_____

_____

_____

_____

_____

_____

_____

_____

_____

_____

_____

_____

_____

DIRECTIONS :

_____

_____

_____

_____

_____

_____

_____

_____

_____

_____

NOTES

_____

_____

_____

_____

RECIPE

DATE : _____

TITLE : _____

PREP TIME : _____

COOK TIME : _____

INGREDIENTS :

_____

_____

_____

_____

_____

_____

_____

_____

_____

_____

_____

_____

_____

_____

DIRECTIONS :

_____

_____

_____

_____

_____

_____

_____

_____

_____

_____

NOTES

_____

_____

_____

RECIPE

DATE : _____

TITLE : _____

PREP TIME : _____

COOK TIME : _____

INGREDIENTS :

_____

_____

_____

_____

_____

_____

_____

_____

_____

_____

_____

_____

_____

_____

_____

DIRECTIONS :

_____

_____

_____

_____

_____

_____

_____

_____

_____

_____

_____

NOTES

_____

_____

_____

RECIPE

DATE : _____

TITLE : _____

PREP TIME : _____

COOK TIME : _____

INGREDIENTS :

_____

_____

_____

_____

_____

_____

_____

_____

_____

_____

_____

_____

_____

_____

_____

_____

DIRECTIONS :

_____

_____

_____

_____

_____

_____

_____

_____

_____

_____

_____

NOTES

_____

_____

_____

_____

RECIPE

DATE : _____

TITLE : _____

PREP TIME : _____

COOK TIME : _____

INGREDIENTS :

_____

_____

_____

_____

_____

_____

_____

_____

_____

_____

_____

_____

_____

_____

_____

DIRECTIONS :

_____

_____

_____

_____

_____

_____

_____

_____

_____

_____

NOTES

_____

_____

_____

_____

RECIPE

DATE : _____

TITLE : _____

PREP TIME : _____

COOK TIME : _____

INGREDIENTS :

_____

_____

_____

_____

_____

_____

_____

_____

_____

_____

_____

_____

_____

_____

_____

_____

_____

DIRECTIONS :

_____

_____

_____

_____

_____

_____

_____

_____

_____

_____

_____

_____

NOTES

_____

_____

_____

_____

RECIPE

DATE : _____

TITLE : _____

PREP TIME : _____

COOK TIME : _____

INGREDIENTS :

_____

_____

_____

_____

_____

_____

_____

_____

_____

_____

_____

_____

_____

_____

_____

_____

DIRECTIONS :

_____

_____

_____

_____

_____

_____

_____

_____

_____

_____

_____

_____

NOTES

_____

_____

_____

_____

RECIPE

DATE : _____

TITLE : _____

PREP TIME : _____

COOK TIME : _____

INGREDIENTS :

_____

_____

_____

_____

_____

_____

_____

_____

_____

_____

_____

_____

_____

_____

_____

_____

DIRECTIONS :

_____

_____

_____

_____

_____

_____

_____

_____

_____

_____

_____

NOTES

_____

_____

_____

_____

RECIPE

DATE : _____

TITLE : _____

PREP TIME : _____

COOK TIME : _____

INGREDIENTS :

_____

_____

_____

_____

_____

_____

_____

_____

_____

_____

_____

_____

_____

_____

_____

_____

DIRECTIONS :

_____

_____

_____

_____

_____

_____

_____

_____

_____

_____

_____

NOTES

_____

_____

_____

_____

RECIPE

DATE : _____

TITLE : _____

PREP TIME : _____

COOK TIME : _____

INGREDIENTS :

_____

_____

_____

_____

_____

_____

_____

_____

_____

_____

_____

_____

_____

_____

_____

DIRECTIONS :

_____

_____

_____

_____

_____

_____

_____

_____

_____

_____

NOTES

_____

_____

_____

_____

RECIPE

DATE : _____

TITLE : _____

PREP TIME : _____

COOK TIME : _____

INGREDIENTS :

_____

_____

_____

_____

_____

_____

_____

_____

_____

_____

_____

_____

_____

_____

_____

DIRECTIONS :

_____

_____

_____

_____

_____

_____

_____

_____

_____

_____

_____

NOTES

_____

_____

_____

_____

RECIPE

DATE : _____

TITLE : _____

PREP TIME : _____

COOK TIME : _____

INGREDIENTS :

_____

_____

_____

_____

_____

_____

_____

_____

_____

_____

_____

_____

_____

_____

_____

_____

DIRECTIONS :

_____

_____

_____

_____

_____

_____

_____

_____

_____

_____

_____

NOTES

_____

_____

_____

_____

RECIPE

DATE : _____

TITLE : _____

PREP TIME : _____

COOK TIME : _____

INGREDIENTS :

_____

_____

_____

_____

_____

_____

_____

_____

_____

_____

_____

_____

_____

_____

_____

DIRECTIONS :

_____

_____

_____

_____

_____

_____

_____

_____

_____

_____

NOTES

_____

_____

_____

_____

RECIPE

DATE : _____

TITLE : _____

PREP TIME : _____

COOK TIME : _____

INGREDIENTS :

_____

_____

_____

_____

_____

_____

_____

_____

_____

_____

_____

_____

_____

_____

DIRECTIONS :

_____

_____

_____

_____

_____

_____

_____

_____

_____

_____

NOTES

_____

_____

_____

_____

RECIPE

DATE : _____

TITLE : _____

PREP TIME : _____

COOK TIME : _____

INGREDIENTS :

_____

_____

_____

_____

_____

_____

_____

_____

_____

_____

_____

_____

_____

_____

_____

_____

_____

DIRECTIONS :

_____

_____

_____

_____

_____

_____

_____

_____

_____

_____

_____

_____

NOTES

_____

_____

_____

_____

RECIPE

DATE : _____

TITLE : _____

PREP TIME : _____

COOK TIME : _____

INGREDIENTS :

_____

_____

_____

_____

_____

_____

_____

_____

_____

_____

_____

_____

_____

_____

_____

DIRECTIONS :

_____

_____

_____

_____

_____

_____

_____

_____

_____

_____

_____

NOTES

_____

_____

_____

_____

RECIPE

DATE : _____

TITLE : _____

PREP TIME : _____

COOK TIME : _____

INGREDIENTS :

_____

_____

_____

_____

_____

_____

_____

_____

_____

_____

_____

_____

_____

_____

_____

_____

DIRECTIONS :

_____

_____

_____

_____

_____

_____

_____

_____

_____

_____

_____

NOTES

_____

_____

_____

_____

RECIPE

DATE : _____

TITLE : _____

PREP TIME : _____

COOK TIME : _____

INGREDIENTS :

_____

_____

_____

_____

_____

_____

_____

_____

_____

_____

_____

_____

_____

_____

_____

DIRECTIONS :

_____

_____

_____

_____

_____

_____

_____

_____

_____

_____

NOTES

_____

_____

_____

_____

RECIPE

DATE : _____

TITLE : _____

PREP TIME : _____

COOK TIME : _____

INGREDIENTS :

_____

_____

_____

_____

_____

_____

_____

_____

_____

_____

_____

_____

_____

_____

_____

_____

DIRECTIONS :

_____

_____

_____

_____

_____

_____

_____

_____

_____

_____

NOTES

_____

_____

_____

_____

RECIPE

DATE : _____

TITLE : _____

PREP TIME : _____

COOK TIME : _____

INGREDIENTS :

_____

_____

_____

_____

_____

_____

_____

_____

_____

_____

_____

_____

_____

_____

_____

_____

DIRECTIONS :

_____

_____

_____

_____

_____

_____

_____

_____

_____

_____

NOTES

_____

_____

_____

_____

RECIPE

DATE : _____

TITLE : _____

PREP TIME : _____

COOK TIME : _____

INGREDIENTS :

_____

_____

_____

_____

_____

_____

_____

_____

_____

_____

_____

_____

_____

_____

DIRECTIONS :

_____

_____

_____

_____

_____

_____

_____

_____

_____

_____

NOTES

_____

_____

_____

_____

RECIPE

DATE : _____

TITLE : _____

PREP TIME : _____

COOK TIME : _____

INGREDIENTS :

_____

_____

_____

_____

_____

_____

_____

_____

_____

_____

_____

_____

_____

_____

DIRECTIONS :

_____

_____

_____

_____

_____

_____

_____

_____

_____

_____

NOTES

_____

_____

_____

_____

RECIPE

DATE : _____

TITLE : _____

PREP TIME : _____

COOK TIME : _____

INGREDIENTS :

_____

_____

_____

_____

_____

_____

_____

_____

_____

_____

_____

_____

_____

_____

_____

_____

DIRECTIONS :

_____

_____

_____

_____

_____

_____

_____

_____

_____

_____

NOTES

_____

_____

_____

_____

RECIPE

DATE : _____

TITLE : _____

PREP TIME : _____

COOK TIME : _____

INGREDIENTS :

_____

_____

_____

_____

_____

_____

_____

_____

_____

_____

_____

_____

_____

_____

_____

_____

DIRECTIONS :

_____

_____

_____

_____

_____

_____

_____

_____

_____

_____

_____

_____

NOTES

_____

_____

_____

_____

RECIPE

DATE : _____

TITLE : _____

PREP TIME : _____

COOK TIME : _____

INGREDIENTS :

_____

_____

_____

_____

_____

_____

_____

_____

_____

_____

_____

_____

_____

_____

_____

DIRECTIONS :

_____

_____

_____

_____

_____

_____

_____

_____

_____

_____

_____

NOTES

_____

_____

_____

_____

RECIPE

DATE : _____

TITLE : _____

PREP TIME : _____

COOK TIME : _____

INGREDIENTS :

_____

_____

_____

_____

_____

_____

_____

_____

_____

_____

_____

_____

_____

_____

_____

DIRECTIONS :

_____

_____

_____

_____

_____

_____

_____

_____

_____

_____

NOTES

_____

_____

_____

_____

RECIPE

DATE : _____

TITLE : _____

PREP TIME : _____

COOK TIME : _____

INGREDIENTS :

_____

_____

_____

_____

_____

_____

_____

_____

_____

_____

_____

_____

_____

_____

_____

_____

DIRECTIONS :

_____

_____

_____

_____

_____

_____

_____

_____

_____

_____

_____

NOTES

_____

_____

_____

_____

RECIPE

DATE : _____

TITLE : _____

PREP TIME : _____

COOK TIME : _____

INGREDIENTS :

_____

_____

_____

_____

_____

_____

_____

_____

_____

_____

_____

_____

_____

_____

_____

_____

DIRECTIONS :

_____

_____

_____

_____

_____

_____

_____

_____

_____

_____

NOTES

_____

_____

_____

_____

RECIPE

DATE : _____

TITLE : _____

PREP TIME : _____

COOK TIME : _____

INGREDIENTS :

_____

_____

_____

_____

_____

_____

_____

_____

_____

_____

_____

_____

_____

_____

_____

DIRECTIONS :

_____

_____

_____

_____

_____

_____

_____

_____

_____

_____

NOTES

_____

_____

_____

_____

RECIPE

DATE : _____

TITLE : _____

PREP TIME : _____

COOK TIME : _____

INGREDIENTS :

_____

_____

_____

_____

_____

_____

_____

_____

_____

_____

_____

_____

_____

_____

_____

DIRECTIONS :

_____

_____

_____

_____

_____

_____

_____

_____

_____

_____

_____

NOTES

_____

_____

_____

_____

RECIPE

DATE : _____

TITLE : _____

PREP TIME : _____

COOK TIME : _____

INGREDIENTS :

_____

_____

_____

_____

_____

_____

_____

_____

_____

_____

_____

_____

_____

_____

_____

DIRECTIONS :

_____

_____

_____

_____

_____

_____

_____

_____

_____

_____

NOTES

_____

_____

_____

_____

RECIPE

DATE : _____

TITLE : _____

PREP TIME : _____

COOK TIME : _____

INGREDIENTS :

_____

_____

_____

_____

_____

_____

_____

_____

_____

_____

_____

_____

_____

_____

_____

_____

DIRECTIONS :

_____

_____

_____

_____

_____

_____

_____

_____

_____

_____

_____

NOTES

_____

_____

_____

_____

RECIPE

DATE : _____

TITLE : _____

PREP TIME : _____

COOK TIME : _____

INGREDIENTS :

_____

_____

_____

_____

_____

_____

_____

_____

_____

_____

_____

_____

_____

_____

_____

DIRECTIONS :

_____

_____

_____

_____

_____

_____

_____

_____

_____

_____

NOTES

_____

_____

_____

_____

RECIPE

DATE : _____

TITLE : _____

PREP TIME : _____

COOK TIME : _____

INGREDIENTS :

_____

_____

_____

_____

_____

_____

_____

_____

_____

_____

_____

_____

_____

_____

_____

DIRECTIONS :

_____

_____

_____

_____

_____

_____

_____

_____

_____

_____

_____

NOTES

_____

_____

_____

RECIPE

DATE : _____

TITLE : _____

PREP TIME : _____

COOK TIME : _____

INGREDIENTS :

_____

_____

_____

_____

_____

_____

_____

_____

_____

_____

_____

_____

_____

_____

_____

_____

DIRECTIONS :

_____

_____

_____

_____

_____

_____

_____

_____

_____

_____

_____

_____

NOTES

_____

_____

_____

_____

RECIPE

DATE : _____

TITLE : _____

PREP TIME : _____

COOK TIME : _____

INGREDIENTS :

_____

_____

_____

_____

_____

_____

_____

_____

_____

_____

_____

_____

_____

_____

_____

_____

DIRECTIONS :

_____

_____

_____

_____

_____

_____

_____

_____

_____

_____

_____

NOTES

_____

_____

_____

_____

RECIPE

DATE : _____

TITLE : _____

PREP TIME : _____

COOK TIME : _____

INGREDIENTS :

_____

_____

_____

_____

_____

_____

_____

_____

_____

_____

_____

_____

_____

_____

_____

DIRECTIONS :

_____

_____

_____

_____

_____

_____

_____

_____

_____

_____

_____

NOTES

_____

_____

_____

_____

RECIPE

DATE : _____

TITLE : _____

PREP TIME : _____

COOK TIME : _____

INGREDIENTS :

_____

_____

_____

_____

_____

_____

_____

_____

_____

_____

_____

_____

_____

_____

_____

_____

DIRECTIONS :

_____

_____

_____

_____

_____

_____

_____

_____

_____

_____

_____

NOTES

_____

_____

_____

_____

RECIPE

DATE : _____

TITLE : _____

PREP TIME : _____

COOK TIME : _____

INGREDIENTS :

_____

_____

_____

_____

_____

_____

_____

_____

_____

_____

_____

_____

_____

_____

_____

DIRECTIONS :

_____

_____

_____

_____

_____

_____

_____

_____

_____

_____

NOTES

_____

_____

_____

_____

RECIPE

DATE : _____

TITLE : _____

PREP TIME : _____

COOK TIME : _____

INGREDIENTS :

_____

_____

_____

_____

_____

_____

_____

_____

_____

_____

_____

_____

_____

_____

_____

_____

DIRECTIONS :

_____

_____

_____

_____

_____

_____

_____

_____

_____

_____

_____

NOTES

_____

_____

_____

_____

RECIPE

DATE : _____

TITLE : _____

PREP TIME : _____

COOK TIME : _____

INGREDIENTS :

_____

_____

_____

_____

_____

_____

_____

_____

_____

_____

_____

_____

_____

_____

_____

_____

DIRECTIONS :

_____

_____

_____

_____

_____

_____

_____

_____

_____

_____

_____

NOTES

_____

_____

_____

_____

RECIPE

DATE : _____

TITLE : _____

PREP TIME : _____

COOK TIME : _____

INGREDIENTS :

_____

_____

_____

_____

_____

_____

_____

_____

_____

_____

_____

_____

_____

_____

_____

_____

DIRECTIONS :

_____

_____

_____

_____

_____

_____

_____

_____

_____

_____

_____

NOTES

_____

_____

_____

RECIPE

DATE : _____

TITLE : _____

PREP TIME : _____

COOK TIME : _____

INGREDIENTS :

_____

_____

_____

_____

_____

_____

_____

_____

_____

_____

_____

_____

_____

_____

_____

DIRECTIONS :

_____

_____

_____

_____

_____

_____

_____

_____

_____

_____

_____

NOTES

_____

_____

_____

_____

RECIPE

DATE : _____

TITLE : _____

PREP TIME : _____

COOK TIME : _____

INGREDIENTS :

_____

_____

_____

_____

_____

_____

_____

_____

_____

_____

_____

_____

_____

_____

_____

_____

DIRECTIONS :

_____

_____

_____

_____

_____

_____

_____

_____

_____

_____

NOTES

_____

_____

_____

_____

RECIPE

DATE : _____

TITLE : _____

PREP TIME : _____

COOK TIME : _____

INGREDIENTS :

_____

_____

_____

_____

_____

_____

_____

_____

_____

_____

_____

_____

_____

_____

_____

_____

DIRECTIONS :

_____

_____

_____

_____

_____

_____

_____

_____

_____

_____

_____

NOTES

_____

_____

_____

_____

RECIPE

DATE : _____

TITLE : _____

PREP TIME : _____

COOK TIME : _____

INGREDIENTS :

_____

_____

_____

_____

_____

_____

_____

_____

_____

_____

_____

_____

_____

_____

_____

_____

DIRECTIONS :

_____

_____

_____

_____

_____

_____

_____

_____

_____

_____

_____

_____

NOTES

_____

_____

_____

_____

RECIPE

DATE : _____

TITLE : _____

PREP TIME : _____

COOK TIME : _____

INGREDIENTS :

_____

_____

_____

_____

_____

_____

_____

_____

_____

_____

_____

_____

_____

_____

_____

_____

DIRECTIONS :

_____

_____

_____

_____

_____

_____

_____

_____

_____

_____

NOTES

_____

_____

_____

_____

RECIPE

DATE : _____

TITLE : _____

PREP TIME : _____

COOK TIME : _____

INGREDIENTS :

_____

_____

_____

_____

_____

_____

_____

_____

_____

_____

_____

_____

_____

_____

_____

_____

DIRECTIONS :

_____

_____

_____

_____

_____

_____

_____

_____

_____

_____

_____

NOTES

_____

_____

_____

RECIPE

DATE : _____

TITLE : _____

PREP TIME : _____

COOK TIME : _____

INGREDIENTS :

_____

_____

_____

_____

_____

_____

_____

_____

_____

_____

_____

_____

_____

_____

DIRECTIONS :

_____

_____

_____

_____

_____

_____

_____

_____

_____

NOTES

_____

_____

_____

_____

RECIPE

DATE : _____

TITLE : _____

PREP TIME : _____

COOK TIME : _____

INGREDIENTS :

_____

_____

_____

_____

_____

_____

_____

_____

_____

_____

_____

_____

_____

_____

DIRECTIONS :

_____

_____

_____

_____

_____

_____

_____

_____

_____

_____

NOTES

_____

_____

_____

_____

RECIPE

DATE : _____

TITLE : _____

PREP TIME : _____

COOK TIME : _____

INGREDIENTS :

_____

_____

_____

_____

_____

_____

_____

_____

_____

_____

_____

_____

_____

_____

_____

DIRECTIONS :

_____

_____

_____

_____

_____

_____

_____

_____

_____

_____

_____

NOTES

_____

_____

_____

_____

_____

RECIPE

DATE : _____

TITLE : _____

PREP TIME : _____

COOK TIME : _____

INGREDIENTS :

_____
_____
_____
_____
_____
_____
_____
_____
_____
_____
_____
_____
_____
_____
_____
_____

DIRECTIONS :

_____
_____
_____
_____
_____
_____
_____
_____
_____
_____
_____

NOTES

_____
_____
_____
_____

RECIPE

DATE : _____

TITLE : _____

PREP TIME : _____

COOK TIME : _____

INGREDIENTS :

_____
_____
_____
_____
_____
_____
_____
_____
_____
_____
_____
_____
_____
_____
_____

DIRECTIONS :

_____
_____
_____
_____
_____
_____
_____
_____
_____
_____

NOTES

_____
_____
_____
_____

RECIPE

DATE : _____

TITLE : _____

PREP TIME : _____

COOK TIME : _____

INGREDIENTS :

_____
_____
_____
_____
_____
_____
_____
_____
_____
_____
_____
_____
_____
_____
_____
_____
_____

DIRECTIONS :

_____
_____
_____
_____
_____
_____
_____
_____
_____
_____
_____

NOTES

_____
_____
_____
_____